First published 2019
by KingFisher Publishing Ltd
NZBN: 9429046616180

Copyright © 2019 KingFisher Publishing Ltd

All rights reserved. No part of this publication may be reproduced, stored in a retrival systems, or transmitted in any form or by any means electronic, mechanical, photocopying, recording, or otherwise, without the prior written consent of the copyright owner.

ISBN: 978-0-473-47756-1
Published in Christchurch, Aotearoa

www.kingfisherpublishing.com

Meditation on Love

Therese Fisher

As you lay here in your bed, you feel a lovely warm fluffy cloud of love fill your body.

This cloud of love fills your head and your shoulders.

Your arms, through your elbows and your wrists. Down into your fingers.

This cloud of love fills your chest and your belly.

Your waist, your hips, and your pelvis.

Bringing love down into your thighs, through your knees, your calves.

Love flows into your feet, and all around your toes.

Lay here for a moment.

Rest your body in this beautiful warm fluffy cloud of love.

Take a deep breath.

You begin to realise that with each breath you breathe out, a little more love flows out into the world.

Your breath fills your room with beautiful warm fluffy love.

All the rooms of your house.
All the people you love living in your home.
All the animals you love who live in your home.

Your breath sends love out into the garden.

Around all the trees, the flowers, the fruits and the vegetables.

Helping them to grow,
to be beautiful and strong.

Your breath sends love out into the city.

Around all the people of the city and to all the people of the world.

Especially to those most in need of love.

So that everyone sleeping tonight is kept warm, and safe, and loved.

Goodnight my darling.

Parents Note:
If you are using this meditation for your child, this meditation is written to be used as part of your child's bedtime routine.

You and your child can also carry the image of Love with you in your hearts through the day.

www.ingramcontent.com/pod-product-compliance
Lightning Source LLC
Chambersburg PA
CBHW041157290426
44108CB00003B/98